J. John

The Easter connection

DISCOVERING A RELATIONSHIP WITH GOD

Published in 2013 by Philo Trust
Witton House, Lower Road, Chorleywood,
Rickmansworth, WD3 5LB, United Kingdom.

www.philotrust.com

British Library Cataloguing in Publication Data

A catalogue record for this book is available from
the British Library

ISBN: 978-0-9573890-6-9

Design by Rachel Fung

Print Management by Verité CM Ltd

Printed in the England

Contents

Introduction

God wants to communicate with us. He came into the world we know, so that we can reconnect with him.

**THIS EASTER,
DO YOU WANT TO KNOW MORE?**

There are so many good things about Easter, but what lies underneath all the extra church services and chocolate eggs? It can be easy to think of Jesus as nothing more than another Jewish rebel executed by the rulers of Israel. But that would be missing something absolutely crucial that can impact and transform our entire lives. Easter is so incredible; it's been celebrated for over 2,000 years.

What is the essence of it?

God wanted humankind to be reconciled with him, but he knew that many were struggling to understand who he was and what he was all about and that sin was in the way. So he sent his Son to earth to reveal himself to us and to open the way for us to know God.

If it was me I'd have been tempted to impress people, given them a display of my power that would have people in awe. But Jesus died on the cross, an apparently defeated man alongside criminals. Nevertheless God wanted us to see how much he loves us and Jesus' death on a cross was not the end of the story. That Jesus was who he had said he was – that he was God in human flesh – was made clear when, on the third day, he rose from the dead and was seen by many of his followers over the following weeks.

So who is this God?

We all have different ideas of what God is like, many of us imagine him as a stern old man, ready to point the finger and tell us off, or as the 'Great Architect' who set the world in motion then sat back and observed us from a distance.

This Easter why not look beyond these things and discover something more about who God really is and exactly how he feels about us. Find out how we lost our connection with God and how our connection can be restored.

1
Losing the connection

In theory, making the connection with God ought to be natural. **GOD WANTS TO COMMUNICATE WITH US:** he is everywhere, all the time. This means that he is never out of range. There is nowhere on earth that we cannot get through to him.

Sometimes at Easter we find it easier to feel his presence and be aware of him, perhaps when we listen to the Easter story again or attend a service on Good Friday or Easter Sunday. Yet the reality is that for most of the year many people find establishing a connection with God very difficult. They may call, but find that the line appears to be dead. There is only silence.

So where is he?

The teaching of Christianity is that God

is there all the time and is willing to answer, but there are some blockages that need to be overcome.

Let's get some background clear first. In the beginning there was perfect communication between human beings and God. When God created the world, he made it perfect. He created men and women to live under his authority and guidance and to enjoy a relationship with him. God's instructions were meant to protect humanity and provide a life of harmony, joy, order and peace. They connected to him in the best possible ways, but this didn't last very long. Instead, human beings chose to ignore God's instructions and to put themselves, rather than him, first in their lives. The brief and blunt biblical word for this is 'sin'. Notice the middle letter of that little word. As the French atheist Albert Camus put it, 'It's the story of my whole life.'

Sin is not just a specific act but also an ingrained selfishness. Sin is the stubborn tendency we all have for choosing to do, say or even think all manner of things that we know are wrong. This pattern of rebellion that started in the distant past has continued in an unbroken pattern to the present day. Every human being that has ever lived – except one – has committed sin. As the Bible says, 'everyone has sinned; we all fall short of God's glorious standard'.[1] That is at the heart of the problem.

We need to realise that sin is deeper, wider and more persistent than we might think. It is *deeper* than we think because we tend to consider issues of good and bad as simply being about visible actions: about those things that we do.

But sin is deeper than we realise, because it includes words, attitudes and thoughts.

Sin is also *wider* than we think, because it is not just a private, personal matter but something that affects our relationships with each other and with the world. We only need to see the news to be reminded that all too often people make choices on the basis of selfishness, cruelty or greed. Sadly, too, we have to admit that sin is *more persistent* than we imagine. Sin is a reality that is so deeply embedded within human nature that no amount of effort or education will remove it from us. It is all-pervasive within us, affecting every part of our being – thoughts, feelings and actions.

How does sin break that precious connection with God?

Imagine you had a mobile phone but it didn't work. Firstly, it could have something to do with the contract. Sometimes our failure to get a signal on our phone has the very simple explanation that we have either broken or ended the terms of our contract. Perhaps we haven't renewed it, or perhaps we have just gone beyond some agreed limit. Now the Bible teaches that God made a similar contract with human beings. The contract had conditions and terms and by rebelling against him *all of us* have broken it. The line is dead because, by sinning, we broke the contract that made the connection possible. The Bible states clearly that breaking this contract is so serious because the breakdown in communication is a symptom of something far worse: the danger of eternal separation from God for those who have failed to keep the contract. It is that finally we shall *perish* or fail to fulfil the purpose for which we were created.

Secondly, there could be something blocking the signal. Have you ever tried to make a call from your mobile, perhaps from indoors and found that you couldn't get through? So you step outside, maybe walk around the corner of the building and suddenly you have a signal. It happens because the obstacle has been removed. Something – a wall, a building or a hill – has blocked the transmission. For human beings sin is that big obstacle that gets in the way between us and God. Our sin has become a barrier between us and God. While it remains, a connection is impossible.

Whichever way you look at it – as a breaking of a contract or as the creation of a barrier – sin has got in the way between us and God and we know the connection is broken. Worse still, we can do nothing ourselves to solve the problem. No amount of good works will help!

2
God's reconnection remedy

SO IF SIN IS THE PROBLEM, WHAT CAN BE DONE ABOUT IT?

We can do very little about the breakdown in relationship. It's too major and too complex. On our own we cannot restore the broken contract or remove the barrier that blocks our vital connection to God. But what we cannot do, God can and does do. The Good News is that God himself has acted to remedy the problem and restore the connection. But it cost him.

The Bible refers to God as Father, Son and Holy Spirit existing in community of being. God is three in one. God is the Father lovingly watching over us. God is the Son walking alongside us. God is the Holy Spirit living within us.

In order to reconnect something that is broken, it is essential to have someone on either side of the breakage. So in a dispute, you may have a meeting between representatives of both sides acting as mediators or negotiators. When it came to re-establishing the connection with human beings we see God adopting the same principle. That's why we celebrate Christmas, because God himself came to earth. God literally humbled himself and became a human being and was born into this world. He came as Jesus the perfect Mediator, someone who was both fully God (and could represent God) and fully human (so could represent humankind). But most especially, this is why we celebrate Easter – it's when Jesus acted on our behalf like a bridge over an un-crossable chasm. If he was not God, then the bridge is down at the other end; if he was not truly human then the bridge is down at our end. But he was fully God and fully human. As such he was entitled to represent both sides.

The four accounts of the life of Jesus that begin the New Testament show from different perspectives how Jesus lived on this earth. The Gospels recount what Jesus said and did. Right from the start he showed the kind of God that he is. He didn't arrive with flashing lights and a huge parade; he was born to a young girl and his first bed was in a stable among the animals. Jesus came in complete humility. But there were many signs that he wasn't just an ordinary baby. Wise men visited Jesus and brought him gifts: gold, frankincense and myrrh. The precious gold symbolised that this baby was a king, the frankincense was a sign he was a priest and the myrrh indicated right from his birth the significance of his death.

As an adult Jesus claimed to be the Messiah or 'Christ', God's long-promised deliverer. He accepted supreme titles without protest, like 'Son of God' and 'Lord', and acknowledged his works, his teaching and his healings and miracles as the work of God.

He did the things that only God could do: ruling over nature, disease, disaster and death.

He claimed final authority in all matters of religion and he pronounced the forgiveness of sins – bypassing the temple, priests and rituals that were supposed to convey this – on his own authority. He set out the highest morality the world has ever seen and, uniquely, he kept that standard totally. No substantiated accusation has come down to us of any inconsistency between what he taught and how he lived

– he practised what he preached.

He alone of all the human beings who have ever lived was without sin. He kept the contract between man and God that we have all broken. He was, quite literally, perfect.

Yet being perfect in an imperfect world is tough, and provocative to others, and Jesus' own people rejected him. The religious leaders of the day couldn't handle the idea that Jesus might actually be who he claimed to be (the Saviour God on earth). Like many human beings, they did not care to get too close to moral perfection. Eventually, the religious leaders created charges against Jesus and, with the aid of political pressure, persuaded a vulnerable but willing foreign ruler to execute him through nailing him to a cross and leaving him to die in the most shameful and dishonourable way possible. And as Jesus died, the Bible tells us that almost everybody, friends and enemies alike, thought that this was the end of the story.

Yet it wasn't. On the third day after the crucifixion, Jesus' tomb was empty and reports began circulating that he had appeared bodily and physically alive to his followers. The appearances were of a solid, living, resurrected human, a being who was now beyond death. The Bible records that Jesus appeared to over 500 people after his resurrection from the dead, over a period of forty days. His followers then and now have seen in the resurrection the living proof that Jesus was everything that he claimed to be: Son of God, Messiah, Lord; the sinless one and the conqueror of death and evil, reversing all the negative verdicts of his enemies against him. After promising his disciples his continued presence through God's Holy Spirit, Jesus returned to heaven after forty days, with his glorified human body – so there's a human in glory, the first or 'firstfruits' of many who will come through death to live again.[2]

The rest of the New Testament tells the amazing story of people who came to God through Jesus. Each person had their story of how God touched their lives in a way that was personal to each and every one. The writers of the New Testament all agree that Jesus' death was no tragic accident, but the very goal of his life. Jesus was born to die.

'Why did Jesus die?' you ask.

In that terrible execution God was, in some extraordinary way, restoring the connection back to himself by fixing everything again.

Perhaps one of the easiest ways of understanding what Jesus achieved on the cross is to think of our serious communications problem. Think first about that illustration of the broken contract. Jesus kept the contract and, through his death on the cross, restored the signal. By being both God and man, Jesus could represent and link both sides of the broken communication chain. The only one who had ever kept the contract took the rap so that the many who had broken the contract could be forgiven and reconnected. Jesus took the penalty that our selfishness deserved.

In Jesus, God himself took on all of human sin and suffered death so that you and I might be forgiven, escape eternal death and have life forever with God.

Through the cross, the contract is renewed for all eternity: we can now have a lasting and secure peace with God. The Bible says: 'Therefore, since we have been made right in God's sight by faith, we have peace with God because of what Jesus Christ our Lord has done for us.'[3] And again: 'Christ suffered for our sins once for all time. He never sinned, but he died for sinners to bring you safely home to God. He suffered physical death, but he was raised to life in the Spirit.'[4]

Now think about that second idea: our sin as a barrier to meaningful communication. One of the many ways of thinking about the cross is that somehow Jesus was taking upon himself the sins of the world. He was confronting the barrier between us and God and demolishing it by his own death. Here the Bible states: 'You were dead because of your sins and because your sinful nature was not yet cut away. Then God made you alive with Christ, for he forgave all our sins. He cancelled the record of the charges against us and took it away by nailing it to the cross.'[5]

3

Getting
reconnected

We have seen that GOD HAS DONE EVERYTHING HE CAN DO TO RESTORE THE LINKS BETWEEN HIMSELF AND US. In Jesus, he has himself stood in the gap between us and personally suffered all the penalties of the contract we have broken and cleared the barrier of sin away to allow a new relationship to commence. The fact that God has done everything for us in such a free and generous manner is what the Bible calls *grace*.

One thing – and only one thing – is needed: we must respond to his grace offered to us. Consider the phone again. Imagine that the problem you have is now fixed: your contract is renewed and the barriers to communication have been taken away. Is that enough? In one sense, yes; but it does you no good until you pick up the phone and use it. Or think of a great present – it may be everything you've ever wanted, but if it's left in its wrappings, what use is it to you?

Now at this point you may hesitate. Perhaps deep down you believe that you are not good enough for God to want to hear from you. You may feel you've made too many mistakes in life and perhaps you've let yourself and others down badly. Be encouraged

– no amount of sin is too great for God to forgive.

He loves you deeply and is eager to welcome you into his family. Consider this Bible verse: 'For God loved the world so much that he gave his one and only Son, so that everyone who believes in him will not perish but have eternal life.'[6] Notice who it is addressed to: *everyone*. That 'everyone' definitely includes you.

Perhaps, though, you feel that if you were to try to follow Jesus you'd soon end by giving it up. As you look back over your life you see far too many failures: diets; New Year's resolutions; promises to yourself and to others. How could this be any different? Well, God knows our frailties and weaknesses and he has given his Holy Spirit to those who have decided to follow Jesus. If you become a Christian and genuinely put your trust in Jesus Christ then God promises he will give you the Holy Spirit to live within you and strengthen you.[7] You can now face the world and all its temptations and problems, not on your own, but with God's own power to help you. It is the task of the Holy Spirit to help us each day to become more like Christ.

He guides us, empowers us and sometimes rebukes us so that we become more like Christ.

And remember, this is not like a New Year's resolution; it is the beginning of a new relationship.

You now might be thinking, what must I do practically to be connected to God? There are three simple steps . . .

4

Making the
connection

If you do indeed want to make a connection with God, you need to take three steps:

ADMIT, COMMIT AND SUBMIT.

1. ADMIT

Either silently or aloud, admit that you have been disconnected from God: that you have broken the contract, and that you have allowed the barrier of sin to separate you from him. Tell God specifically about those areas of your life where you've messed up. Remember, there is no point in blaming others or trying to conceal anything. He knows everything already. He just wants you to own up to it. So, tell God how sorry you are.

2. COMMIT

Think about Jesus, dying on the cross for you. Remember that he bore the responsibility for the contract you broke and that he took upon himself the barrier of sin you had created, and then demolished it. Through Jesus, God has dealt permanently and completely with your sin. You can now be totally forgiven for everything you ever have done wrong. Thank God for what Jesus has done for you and tell God that you accept his forgiveness, and that you commit your life to him, for him to remake and fully restore it. This includes seeking to discover his will for your life now, and the part you'll get to play in restoring his broken world and other people's broken lives too.

3. SUBMIT

Thirdly, choose to submit the whole of your life to the God of love. You are beginning a new relationship with him, and with others, in God's new community. Ask him to help you to live out this relationship day by day. Submitting to God involves choosing to live a life that pleases him and starting to behave in right ways. Remember that submitting your life to God and living for him is not something that you are expected to handle alone. God knows that we would find this an almost impossible task and that is why he gives us his Holy Spirit and his church – restored power and restored people just like you.

A PRAYER

Pray these words, which clearly and concisely capture the essence of the Easter Connection:

Thank you, God, for loving me before I ever loved you.

Thank you, Jesus, for dying on the cross, for me.

Thank you that I can get connected to you now because you are alive today.

I admit that I have lived my life without you and have messed up.

I ask for your total forgiveness and I commit myself to you.

Help me to submit my life to your teaching and direction from now on.

I receive you into my life and ask you to fill me with your Holy Spirit.
Amen.

WELCOME, you are now connected and now it is vital that you stay connected.

5
Staying connected

Being a Christian is not just something to think about at Easter.

IT'S THE BEGINNING OF A LIFELONG JOURNEY AND ADVENTURE.

The Bible talks about the experience of coming to faith in Christ as being 'born again'.[8] That's a great image, but no one wants to stay a baby. The key thing to living the Christian life is to keep growing in your relationship with God. We have used the illustration of phones in this book because it's important to get your priorities in line with God's priority. You would be a pretty sad person to rate your phone as being more important than the friends you use it to contact. People and relationships are always much more important than things. It's the same with the Christian life: it's the relationship with God that is the important thing. Now that you are reconnected, you need to *stay* connected. Let me suggest one basic principle and four vital practices to help.

A BASIC PRINCIPLE

The way the Bible explains it, becoming a Christian is not like signing up with a phone company, it's more like being adopted into a new family.[9] We were once far away from God, completely separated from him by our sin and failure to keep the contract. But now, thanks to what Christ did for us, we are God's children and he is our perfect heavenly parent. That is an absolutely essential principle that we need to hold on to because it gives us confidence in our relationship with God. A company might disconnect you, a club might kick you out but no good parent would ever reject their child and certainly not God, the perfect parent. He is now our loving and totally committed heavenly Father, unlike some earthly fathers, who may have failed and disappointed us. We are his and we will stay his forever.

The principle that Christianity is about being adopted into God's family should guide you in how you live. You don't have to earn his love, or top up your credit with him by behaving in 'religious' ways.

God loves you because you are his and he will never give up on you.

There is a great phrase about God in Psalm 136 that is repeated 26 times: 'His faithful love endures forever.'

God, the perfect heavenly parent, delights in giving good things to his children. In this life and the next you are likely to be constantly surprised by God's goodness to you and his surprise gifts and generosity. Don't forget to thank him.

FOUR VITAL PRACTICES

There are four ways to build our relationship with God. We can read about him in the Bible, we can communicate with him through prayer, we can meet with others who follow him and we can share what we know about Christ with others. These four things are vital to keeping that good relationship going and growing.

1. Reading the Bible

The Bible is a library of sixty-six short books, all in one volume – some history, some prophecy, some poetry and some letters to individuals and communities, all written over fifteen hundred years by many different authors.

Christians believe that there is a dual authorship to Scripture: men and women spoke and God spoke through them – a fully divine and authentically human word from God.

Perhaps the best summary of what the Bible is about comes from the Bible itself: 'All Scripture is inspired by God and is useful to teach us what is true and to make us realise what is wrong in our lives. It corrects us when we are wrong and teaches us to do what is right. God uses it to prepare and equip his people to do every good work.'[10]

Although originally written in Hebrew, Aramaic and Greek, the Bible has always been translated into other languages for access to all. I urge you to have a good and modern translation, such as the New Living Translation or the New International Version, and begin a good habit of regular reading. If you are not familiar with the Bible, the Gospel of John in the New Testament is a good place to start. The other Gospels and the New Testament letters are also books that you should read. There are a number of good Study Bibles with insightful commentaries and notes that help you understand the background and meaning to particular passages and these can be very valuable. As you read the Bible it is good to pray that God's Spirit would help you both understand what you are reading and apply it to your own life.

Above all, treat the Bible seriously. The Bible is the world's best-selling book for good reason: through it we hear God communicating directly with us. Read it attentively and your life will be transformed.

2. Praying to God

No relationship flourishes without communication and our relationship with God is no exception. Prayer needs to be regular, honest and wide-ranging. Do not be afraid to bring apparently insignificant things to God.

If you are not sure how to go about praying, take a look at the prayer below

– you may be familiar with it. This is what Jesus taught his disciples when they asked him how to pray.

Our Father in heaven, may your name be kept holy.

May your Kingdom come soon.

May your will be done on earth, as it is in heaven.

Give us today the food we need, and forgive us our sins, as we have forgiven those who sin against us.

And don't let us yield to temptation, but rescue us from the evil one.[11]

- The first phrase of the prayer ('Our Father in heaven, may your name be kept holy') expresses how great God is, and reminds us that he is holy and the focus of true worship. It is good to begin our prayers by thanking

God and remembering his goodness and grace.

- The second phrase of the prayer ('May your Kingdom come soon') reminds us of what should be our greatest priority: the rule of God over this world that he created. That takes precedence over our own needs, however urgent they may be.

- The third phrase ('May your will be done on earth, as it is in heaven') is a reminder that for our relationship with God to be in any sort of healthy shape we need to do what he wants. There is an important element in prayer of seeking God's will for our lives, and also for the big-picture unfolding of world history.

- With the fourth phrase ('Give us today the food we need'), we ask

God to provide for all our needs, whether they are for provision, peace or protection.

- In the fifth phrase Jesus turns to forgiveness ('and forgive us our sins, as we have forgiven those who sin against us'). There are always words, deeds and thoughts that we need to ask God's forgiveness for. It's helpful to regularly acknowledge where we have hurt God, someone else or ourselves. If we confess these things and seek God's forgiveness the Bible assures us that we will receive forgiveness. As the Bible says, 'If we confess our sins to him [God], he is faithful and just to forgive us our sins and to cleanse us from all wickedness.'[12] Interestingly, the prayer makes the point that we must not be simply receivers of forgiveness. Just as we receive forgiveness from God, so we must forgive others. The forgiven are to forgive – totally, or they will jeopardise their assurance of God's forgiveness themselves. Bitterness, resentment and unforgiveness are real soul-killers.[13]

• With the sixth phrase ('And don't let us yield to temptation, but rescue us from the evil one') we pray that we would not be tested or tempted beyond our endurance. The Bible makes it clear that this world is not neutral territory. There are temptations – and a tempter – that we need to resist. We need to have God's strength in order to live in ways that consistently honour him.

Try and spend time each day talking to God in prayer alone, and with others, when possible. Some people prefer to pray silently, others have the privacy to pray audibly and others write their prayers down in a journal.

Start by praying for just a few minutes, and you'll soon find that you're inspired to spend longer in the presence of such a good, loving, gracious God.

You will experience many amazing answers from him.

3. Having community with others

When you became a Christian you were adopted as one of God's children and are now part of the community of God. This has an interesting implication. We have not simply gained a loving heavenly Father, but also other brothers and sisters. The Christian life is meant to be communal, not solitary.

Joining a church community is vital. Through it you will meet with other people who know and love God and you will find out more about him and grow in faith. The Bible says this: 'And let us not neglect our meeting together, as some people do, but encourage one another, especially now that the day of his return is drawing near.'[14]

There is no such thing as solitary Christianity, for God wants true community.

In the church community, you will be

able to worship God in a new way –
to give expression along with others
to the joy and thankfulness in your
heart. You will receive teaching to
inspire, challenge and encourage you.
So get involved. Your church may
run groups during the week where
Christians meet for fellowship, food,
prayer, Bible study and social concern.
You will find them invaluable.

It is important to remember that church
is not a cruise liner on which we glide
our way to heaven on permanent
vacation. It is a battleship that requires
all hands on deck as it fights its way
to a glorious destination. Indeed, it
is a vital principle of Christianity that
although we are rescued by grace,
you get out of the Christian life what
you put in. The best way to be truly
blessed is to work at being a blessing

to others. You will, I'm sure, find that the church you get involved with will need helpers (I've never known one that didn't) and I urge you to volunteer with your natural and spiritual gifts.

Whether it's with children, youth or the elderly, serving those in need or just serving coffee, it's important that we serve.

If we aren't faithful with little things, God rarely trusts us with bigger things.

4. Sharing the Good News of Jesus with others

We receive the Holy Spirit, not to stagnate like the Dead Sea without any outlet, but to overflow to benefit others. We need to communicate our faith both visibly and verbally. Jesus said, 'You are the light of the world.'[15] The witness of a light in a dark place speaks for itself. So become intentional in praying, caring and sharing with those people with whom you naturally interact in your world.

6

God's on
the line

Perhaps this Easter you have made a connection with God for the first time. If you have begun a relationship with God, very soon you will notice a change.

GOD WILL START TO WORK BY HIS HOLY SPIRIT ILLUMINATING YOUR MIND AND HEART TO NEW THINGS AND TEACHING YOU TO LIVE FOR HIM.

I wish I could promise you a trouble-free life as a Christian but Christ did not, and I cannot. The Christian life is not easy. You will need to work at staying connected to God. There is an enemy, the devil, who will do all he can to disrupt your connection with God. Your friends and family may not support your choice to be a Christian and at times it may feel as though the whole world is against you.

Yet God is always there for you and always listening. At times, it may seem as if God is a long way away and you may feel on your own, but I assure you that God is present. When you go through tough times, God may seem closer than ever before. If this is not your experience, be assured that he is still, and will always be, present with you and there for you. Persevere through the hardships you face, because you now have eternal life to look forward to and with God our pain is never wasted. 'We can rejoice, too, when we run into problems and trials, for we know that they help us develop endurance. And endurance develops strength of character, and character strengthens our confident hope of salvation. And this hope will not lead to disappointment. For we know how dearly God loves us, because he has given us the Holy Spirit to fill our hearts with his love.'[16]

Don't give up on reading the Bible, communicating with God through prayer, having fellowship with other Christians and sharing your faith with others. You will need these things to help sustain your faith in the years ahead.

You are not on your own. Millions have gone before you and millions are with you.

Let me encourage you to be confident. Remember that if you have accepted Jesus and committed your life to him, you can have complete assurance that your relationship with God is restored.

Remember:

God is with you.
God loves you.
God will never leave you.
God will be with you forever.

May God grant you the light of Christ,
which is faith;
The warmth of Christ, which is love;
The radiance of Christ,
which is purity;
The belief in Christ, which is truth.

End Notes

1. Romans 3:23
2. 1 Corinthians 15:20 (NIV)
3. Romans 5:1
4. 1 Peter 3:18
5. Colossians 2:13–14
6. John 3:16
7. Acts 2:38; Romans 5:5; 8:11; Galatians 4:6
8. John 1:12–13; 3:3; 1 Peter 1:23
9. Romans 8:15–16; Galatians 4:4–5; 1 John 3:1
10. 2 Timothy 3:16–17
11. Matthew 6:9–13
12. 1 John 1:9
13. Matthew 6:14–15
14. Hebrews 10:25
15. Matthew 5:14
16. Romans 5:3–5

**For additional resources from J.John
visit: www.philotrust.com**

**Twitter: CanonJJohn
Facebook: J.John**